Baking Sourdough Bread

Baking Sourdough Bread

Dozens of Recipes for
Artisan Loaves, Crackers,
and Sweet Breads

Göran Söderin and George Strachal

Photography by Helén Pe I Translated by Malou Fickling

Skyhorse Publishing

10 9 8 7 6 5 4 3 2 1

Library of Congress Cataloging-in-Publication Data

Söderin, Göran.
    [Baka surdegsbrod. English]
    Baking sourdough bread : dozens of recipes for artisan loaves, crackers, and sweet breads / Goran Soderin and George Strachal ; photography by Helen Pe ; translated by Malou Fickling.
        pages cm
    Includes index.
    ISBN 978-1-62636-399-1
1. Sourdough bread. I. Strachal, George. II. Pe, Helén. III. Title.
    TX770.S66S6313 2014
    641.81'57—dc23
                                        2013034019

Printed in China

Contents

The Mystical Sourdough

Sourdough is a divine creation—at least, if you believe what the Bible says about it: "The kingdom of heaven is like unto leaven, which a woman took, and hid in three measures of meal, till the whole was leavened" (*Matthew 13:33*).

The Israelites fled Egypt in a hurry. They didn't have enough time to let the bread rise, meaning they had to bake unleavened bread. Jews celebrate this during the Feast of Unleavened Bread, *Hag HaMatzah*, during which you eat *matzo*—a flat bread baked with flour, oil, salt, and water—for a period of seven days.

When Emperor Augustus ruled the Roman Empire (around the time of the birth of Christ), Rome had over three hundred bakeries that supplied bread to its citizens—bread that was mainly baked with leaven. The largest bakery produced over 100,000 loaves a day. When the Roman Empire collapsed, the major supply bakeries did as well. We don't know much about what happened next. There are few records that tell us of the significance of bread over the years; however, recipes have been found from thirteenth-century monasteries.

According to American literature, the Wild West could never have been conquered without sourdough starters, and the old veterans of Alaska—prospectors and settlers—were called "sourdoughs." They always carried a bit of sourdough in their knapsacks or in a bag that hung from a ribbon around their necks. Unlike yeast, sourdough could keep for long periods of time. You would bring it from home with you in order to obtain the specific taste of the bread you grew up with. Being called "sourdough" was proof of manhood. It meant that you were tough, experienced, and hardened.

Sourdough was valued so highly that it was preserved in the family as if it were worth its weight in gold. Primarily in the United States, the culture around sourdough has created a variety of modern myths. One of the most mystical sourdough cultures is called "The San Francisco Sourdough," and it is made from a lactic acid bacterium called *Lactobacillus sanfransiscensis*. Other types of dough have also been praised in modern sourdough history; these include the German *Sauerteig*, the Russian *Zakvaska*, the Flemish *Desem,* and the French *Levain*.

Back in the olden days, sourdough was believed to serve many functions. The dough was sometimes used as dog food; it could heal wounds, particularly burns; and it was used to make alcoholic beverages. The traditional Russian drink *kvass*, for example, is made from sourdough black or rye bread. The dough could even be used to seal cracks in poorly built houses and to half-sole shoes.

One thing is certain: Sourdough is extremely healthy. Several scientific reports, from foreign as well as national research, demonstrate sourdough's health benefits. One relevant finding is that if you eat sourdough bread in the morning, it's much easier to keep your GI index in balance throughout the day. The lactic acid also helps you get an extra dose of B vitamins. Additionally, there is an increase in acetylcholines—neurotransmitters that affect particular parts of the nervous system. Our blood pressure drops, and we become calmer.

There are tons of recipes and descriptions on how to get a sourdough started and how the bread should be baked. Some are tremendously complex with elaborate instructions when it comes to weight and volume. Usually the description depends on the baker's understanding of the biochemical process that results in the sourdough.

The Chemistry

Someone once said that bread production, and consequently the making of sourdough, was one of mankind's first successful biochemical experiments. Humans had learned to control natural chemical processes.

The fermentation process can be activated by bacteria as well as yeast. This is how it works: Everywhere around us, there are bacteria that are useful in different ways. In fact, every person's body contains a few pounds of bacteria. We would never be able to cope with life on Earth without it. In short, one can say that bacteria are primarily beneficial to humans. Actually, there are many more beneficial bacteria than harmful ones.

Lactobacillus is the bacteria family that plays the lead role in the process of creating a good sourdough.

Opposite page, bottom left: Levain, recipe page 35.

This bacteria can produce both lactic and acetic acid. There are many variations of *lactobacillus*. However, they aren't all suitable for sourdough baking; some are better for making yogurt, buttermilk, or even salami and smoked sausage. Sourdough bread also tastes different in every part of the world; it can even vary within the space of a city, as each variety of *lactobacillus* makes for a unique taste.

Yeast is all over as well. You can find wild yeast on fruits, vegetables, and grains. The more carbohydrates, the higher the concentration of yeast. In this book, we don't explore wild yeast baking in detail, but there are instructions on how to make your own yeast from raisins.

Nature provides numerous varieties of yeasts, but the most common in sourdough is *Saccharomyces exiguus*. What distinguishes conventional baking yeast, *Saccharomyces cerevisiac*, from sourdough yeast is that it's difficult for conventional baking yeast to survive in an acidic environment. By contrast, *S. exiguus* thrives there.

An acidic environment has several advantages. One is that sourdough bread keeps fresher for longer without any added preservatives. Thus, sourdough is a preservative in itself.

What the bacteria and yeast have in common is that they survive on carbohydrates. There are plenty of carbohydrates in flour. One single gram of flour can contain tens of thousands of yeast cells. In order to be able to use the carbohydrates for nutrition so the yeast cells can grow and multiply, it's necessary to add water so the flour starch can break down into sugars. So when we're mixing the water and flour, we start "feeding" the bacteria and yeasts.

The Ingredients

Saving a piece of the sourdough when you are baking is the easiest way to ensure that you can bake bread in the future that is similar to what you are baking now. Back in the olden days, it was common practice to let dough rise in the dough trough. When the dough had been used for the day's baking, there would always be some leftover dough in the trough. All you would have to do was re-fill it with water and flour to start the leavening—that is, the fermentation.

Sourdough is primarily associated with the baking of rye bread, but in southern European bread cultures there are amazing white breads based on wheat flour sourdough.

In this book, we also offer a variety of highly unusual sourdough recipes based on oats, lentils, and potatoes.

Water is key to the creation of sourdough, which is essentially based on the interaction of flour and water. Once you learn how this works, you can try other ways of influencing the bread's taste and texture. If your water contains high levels of chlorine, you should let it stand in an open pitcher in the refrigerator overnight. Chlorine is an element that kills microorganisms such as bacteria and yeasts. Use pure spring water if possible.

Flour is extremely important. Feel free to use whole-wheat flour. This includes bits of chaff from the grain, which contains minerals that both bacterium and yeasts like.

Use organic flour as well. Other types of flour may contain substances that kill or affect the microorganisms, and you won't end up with the sourdough you were expecting. In addition, organic whole-wheat flour is healthier for you.

The gluten content must not be too high. Don't use so-called "strong flour," as it's intended to create large and fluffy bread. The high levels of proteins, including gluten, signal that the flour contains less starch, and it's the starch that microorganisms need in order to reproduce and make the dough rise.

Rye flour is the most common flour when baking sourdough bread in Germany, Russia, and Finland, among other countries. This flour has a very small share of gluten proteins, which, in wheat, help the bread to stay in one piece so it can rise easily. Rye, on the other hand, is rich in a dietary fiber called pentoses. Pentoses attract liquid and help the dough to swell. An acidic environment also means that the pentoses absorb liquids more easily. Rye bread that is baked with sourdough isn't as sticky as bread baked with yeast alone.

Rye flour also has a higher fiber and mineral content than several other flours. This helps with the sourdough process. Additionally, rye flour has higher levels of sugar and amylase. The sugar nourishes the microorganisms, and the amylase—which is an enzyme—is a type of protein that makes the sourdough bread moist.

Wheat flour does not have the same composition as rye flour, but it can still be used to make sourdough. In this case, there are other members of the *lactobacillus* family that make the dough rise. The *Sanfranciscensis* bacteria is important, as well as a yeast called *Candida milleri*. These can be found in rye sourdough as well, but there they play a smaller role. The yeast in wheat dough mainly helps the dough rise, so the gluten proteins can create a network that allows the bread to rise considerably.

In order to produce proper sourdough, the wheat flour you use should be whole wheat. The same goes for spelt wheat. You can certainly make sourdough using sifted flour, but it will take longer. Minerals in the chaff contribute to the comfort of the microorganisms. And compared to rye flour, wheat flour has fewer free sugars. Alpha, a certain type of amylase found in wheat sourdough, is more active and plays a significant role in increasing the sugar content so that *lactobacilli* and yeasts can multiply.

Oat flour is still an uncommon flour for making sourdough. Different varieties of *lactobacillus* and yeast play a significant role here, too.

The fact is that with the help of bacteria, most things that contain carbohydrates can rise. For example, it's possible to make sourdough from flour made of beans, lentils, and potatoes. This book includes a few of these recipes.

Salt, when added to the mixture, will slow down the fermenting process. This means that if you don't have much time, you might need to postpone your baking plans. The addition of salt reduces the activity of the lactic acid bacterwia. To make a normal-sized dough that will yield several loaves, you'll need a couple of teaspoons of salt. In sourdough bread, salt is typically added at the end of the kneading process.

> **More on flour and salt**
> - Whole-grain flour simplifies the production of sourdough.
> - Sifted flour can also be used, but may require a longer baking time.
> - If used in a large quantity, salt can stop the fermentation of the dough altogether. However, a small amount of salt is generally added directly to the dough.

The Process

Sourdough is much more sensitive than other types of dough. Therefore, it's preferable to make them by hand. However, if you choose to use a mixer, keep to a very low speed.

Try to be careful when shaping the loaves—especially when using wheat sourdough. Shape the dough gently with your knuckles (instead of using your whole hand) to preserve the bubbles in the dough and ensure that you get bread that's light and fluffy.

Before You Start

When making sourdough, all ingredients should be at room temperature. Lactic acid bacteria react differently to heat. The ideal temperature for a sourdough culture is about 85°F (30°C). Sourdough cultures tend to become more acidic at a temperature of 70°F (20°C) and milder at a temperature of around 95°F (35°C). This is because the "heterofermentative lactic acid bacteria" starts to produce more acid when it's cooler. At higher temperatures, the "homofermentative lactic acid bacteria" are activated; this bacteria only produces lactic acid. Therefore, the cooler it is, the more acidic the sourdough will be.

When stored in temperatures above 105°F (40°C), the sourdough culture tends to deteriorate. When making a sourdough starter for the first time, put the jar with the flour and water mixture in the oven; just turn on the oven light—no heat. This will slow the growth process down and will maintain a temperature of 75–95°F (25–35°C).

> **The right temperature for sourdough culture**
> - A good temperature for sourdough is around 85°F (30°C).
> - Temperatures above 105°F (40°C) will jeopardize the fermentation.
> - The dough becomes more acidic below 75°F (25°C).

Proportions A few basic ground rules to bear in mind when baking with sourdough:

To make a sourdough starter = 2 parts flour + 2 parts water.

To feed the starter = 1 part water + 1 part flour.

To bake bread = 1 part sourdough starter + 2 parts bread dough.

(There is room for experimentation; for an example, see the recipe for Spelt Sourdough on page 45.)

The Golden Rules

The rising time for sourdough bread is always much longer than for yeast breads.

If you add a little yeast to the dough, you'll get a larger bread with a less sour taste. A "normal" dough for one family requires ⅓–¾ oz (10–20 g) fresh yeast.

An active sourdough will bubble. If it doesn't, it has probably been left standing too long after the last feeding. In this case, feed the leaven again and wait about six hours until it wakes up again. If the sourdough has black streaks or smells rotten, it should be discarded.

A Note on Conversions

As is often the case when a book has been translated from a European language to American English, amounts must be converted from metric into the English System of Measurements. For the ease of American bakers, some of the US measurements included with the recipes have been rounded slightly. For more precise baking, use a kitchen scale to follow the metric measurements.

Making a Sourdough

Rye Sourdough
¾ cup (200 ml) water, room temperature
2 cups (200 g) finely ground rye flour
½ cup (100 g) grated apple, peeled

Combine the ingredients and let stand for 2–4 days in a glass jar with a tight-fitting lid. Stir in the mornings and evenings.

   The starter is ready when the mixture starts to bubble. From this point on, all you have to do is "feed" the dough so that it retains its flavor and ability to ferment. If you leave the sourdough in the refrigerator, you should feed it once a week with ½ cup (100 ml) water and 1 cup (100 g) rye flour. If you keep the sourdough at room temperature, it should be fed every day, in the same manner. The consistency should resemble thick porridge.

   If you have sourdough left over, you can freeze it in containers that hold half a cup or leave a part of it to dry (see page 25).

Wheat or Spelt Sourdough
¾ cup (200 ml) water, room temperature
2 cups (325 g) wheat flour or spelt flour, sifted
½ cup (100 g) grated apple, peeled

Combine the ingredients and let stand for 2–4 days in a glass jar with a tight-fitting lid. Stir in the mornings and evenings.

   The starter is ready when the mixture starts to bubble. From this point on, all you have to do is "feed" the dough so that it retains its flavor and ability to ferment. If you leave the sourdough in the refrigerator, you should feed it once a week with ½ cup (100 ml) water and 1 cup (100 g) wheat flour. If you keep the sourdough at room temperature, it should be fed every day, in the same manner. The consistency should resemble thick porridge.

   If you have sourdough left over, you can freeze it in containers that hold half a cup or leave a part of it to dry (see page 25).

Oat Sourdough

1 cup (200 ml) rolled oats
¼ cup (50 ml) water, room temperature
2 apples, peeled and grated

Mix the oats in a blender until they reach a consistency similar to flour.

Combine the ingredients and let stand for 2–4 days in a glass jar with a tight-fitting lid. Stir in the mornings and evenings.

The starter is ready when the mixture starts to bubble. From this point on, all you have to do is "feed" the dough so that it retains its flavor and ability to ferment. If you leave the sourdough in the refrigerator, you should feed it once a week with ½ cup (100 ml) water and 1 cup (100 g) oat flour. If you keep the sourdough at room temperature, it should be fed every day, in the same manner. The consistency should resemble thick porridge.

If you have sourdough left over, you can freeze it in containers that hold half a cup.

Potato Sourdough

2 medium sized potatoes, peeled
1 tsp honey
1 tbsp spelt flour, sifted

Mix the potatoes until they resemble gruel. Stir in the honey and spelt flour.

Store the mixture in a jar with a tight-fitting lid. Stir in the mornings and evenings.

This sourdough usually takes a little longer to make than others, but it is definitely worth the extra time. It will take 5–7 days before it's done.

The starter is ready when the mixture starts to bubble. From this point on, all you have to do is "feed" the dough so that it retains its flavor and ability to ferment. If you leave the sourdough in the refrigerator, you should feed it once a week with ½ cup (100 ml) potato gruel and 1 tbsp spelt flour. If you keep the sourdough at room temperature, it should be fed every day, in the same manner. The consistency should resemble thick porridge.

If you have sourdough left over, you can freeze it in containers that hold half a cup.

Lentil Sourdough

Day 1
½ cup (100 ml) dried green lentils
½ cup (100 ml) water, room temperature
1 tbsp spelt flour, sifted

With a hand blender, mix the lentils until they begin to resemble flour. Add water and spelt flour.

Pour the mixture into a jar with a tight-fitting lid.

Day 2
½ cup (100 ml) water, room temperature

Add the water. Mix well and let stand in the glass jar for 2–4 days. Stir in the mornings and evenings.

The starter is ready when the mixture starts to bubble. From this point on, all you have to do is "feed" the dough so that it retains its flavor and ability to ferment. If you leave the sourdough in the refrigerator, you should feed it once a week with ½ cup (100 ml) water and 1 cup (100 g) lentil flour, which is equivalent to approximately ⅔ cup (150 ml) lentils. If you keep the sourdough at room temperature, it should be fed every day, in the same manner. The consistency should resemble thick porridge.

If you have sourdough left over, you can freeze it in containers that hold half a cup.

Wild Yeast

Cover the bottom of a glass jar with organic raisins. Add lukewarm water so that nearly two-thirds of the jar is filled. Secure with a tight-fitting lid.

Shake the jar twice a day.

Leave the jar at room temperature for about 6–7 days until noticeable yeast bubbles appear. The initial process may vary depending on the temperature of the room.

Stir the mixture. Place in an airtight jar and let stand for 3 days at room temperature.

Wild yeast is generally used in the same way as ordinary yeast, but remember that it will take longer to ferment, as you use twice the amount of wild yeast as you do regular yeast.

Storing Sourdough

When storing the sourdough starter, it should be fed in the manner previously described, either once a day at room temperature or once a week if it is refrigerated.

You can also dry your sourdough. Place a sheet of parchment paper on a baking sheet. Cover it with a thin layer of the sourdough starter (1–2 mm). Place it in the oven and turn on the oven light. Leave it in the oven until the sourdough has dried completely (this will take between twelve and twenty hours). Then crumble the dry dough, place it in a jar, and cover with a lid. Store the jar at room temperature in a dry environment.

When you're ready to bake, mix a few tablespoons of the dry dough with 1 cup (200 ml) water and 1½ cups (200 g) flour. The next day, you'll have an "activated sourdough starter."

Recipes

Bread with Wheat Sourdough

Italiano

Plan ahead for a bread that's lovely with Saturday meals.

Makes 3 loaves

Day 1
⅔ cup (150 g) water, room temperature
2 cups (250 g) wheat flour
1 ¾ tsp (5 g) fresh yeast

Mix the ingredients well. Let the dough rise in the refrigerator for about 12 hours.

Day 2
9 cups (1.1 kg) wheat flour
2 cups (500 ml) water, room temperature
12 oz (350 g) wheat sourdough starter (see page 20)
½–1 tbsp honey
½ tbsp (10 g) salt

Add all ingredients except the salt to the dough that was prepared the previous day. Knead until elastic and add the salt.

Split the dough into three parts and shape into round loaves. Gently dip the loaves in flour and place on a greased baking sheet.

Let the loaves rise in the refrigerator for about 10 hours.

Bake the loaves at 475°F (240°C) for 25–30 minutes.

Rosemary Bread

This bread goes well with soup.

Makes 1 loaf

3 oz (80 g) wheat sourdough starter (see page 20)
2 cups (250 g) wheat flour
½ cup (125 ml) water, room temperature
3½ tsp (10 g) fresh yeast
1 tsp (5 g) salt
1 tbsp olive oil
fresh rosemary

Mix all the ingredients, except the oil and rosemary, until you have a smooth dough. Let it rise for 20 minutes.

Roll out the dough and shape it into a rectangle that is about one-tenth of an inch (3 mm) thick.

Brush with olive oil. Chop the rosemary and sprinkle on top of the dough. Then, roll the dough up from the short side of the rectangle. Secure the ends.

Let the bread rise for about 30 minutes and score a deep incision in the center of the dough roll so that all the layers are visible. Let it rise for another 10 minutes.

Initial oven temperature: 475°F (250°C)
Place the bread in the oven. Sprinkle a cup of water onto the bottom of the oven. Lower the temperature to 400°F (210°C) and bake for about 20 minutes.

Brush the dough with oil and spread the rosemary evenly on top.

Roll the dough up. Pinch the ends of together.

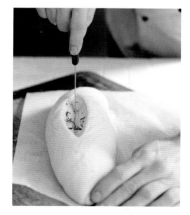

Score the bread after it has risen.

Cheese and Sesame Bread

This bread is so flavorful that it should be eaten without any spreads or extras.

Makes 3 loaves

Day 1
8½ oz (240 g) wheat sourdough starter (see page 20)
1½ cup (350 ml) water, room temperature
1½ cup (200 g) durum wheat flour
1½ cup (200 g) wheat flour

Mix the ingredients thoroughly and let rise in the refrigerator for about 12 hours.

Day 2
1 tbsp (15 g) salt
2¼ cup (250 g) grated cheese, such as aged Swiss or Emmental
½ cup (100 ml) toasted sesame seeds
3⅓ cups (400 g) wheat flour (amount will vary depending on the cheese used)
olive oil for the bowl

Remove the dough from the refrigerator well in advance to ensure that it isn't too cold. Add salt, cheese, sesame seeds, and flour. The drier the cheese, the less flour you'll need. Mix well and let rise in a greased mixing bowl covered with tin foil until the dough has doubled in size.

Carefully spread the dough out on a table and cut it into thirds. Gently shape into round loaves. Place the loaves on a greased baking sheet and let the bread rise for approximately 30 minutes.

Initial Oven Temperature: 450°F (230°C)
Put the bread in the oven and reduce the temperature to 400°F (210°C). Bake for about 30 minutes.

Toast the sesame seeds in a dry pan. Leave the sesame seeds to cool before mixing the dough.

When the dough is ready, carefully shape into round loaves.

After the loaves have risen for thirty minutes, flour and gently make incisions on top of the loaves before placing them in the oven.

Levain

France's classic white sourdough bread.

Makes 2 loaves

Day 1
3½ oz (100 g) wheat sourdough starter (see page 20)
1 cup (200 ml) water, room temperature
1¼ cup (150 g) wheat flour
½ cup (50 g) unmixed rye flour (i.e., flour without wheat)

Mix all the ingredients well.

Place the dough in a bowl and cover it with cling wrap. Store it in the refrigerator overnight.

Day 2
2 cups (450 ml) water, room temperature
6 cups (750 g) wheat flour
4 tsp (20 g) sea salt

Add water and flour to the dough. Knead well. Add the salt. Knead the dough for another 2 minutes.

Let rise for 1 hour and then gently shape into two loaves.

Let the loaves rise under a cloth for 45 minutes.

Initial Oven Temperature: 525°F (280°C)
Put the loaves in the oven. Sprinkle a cup of water on the bottom of the oven. Reduce the temperature to 450°F (230°C) and bake for 30 minutes.

Carefully pour the dough onto a floured surface. Divide it into two parts.

Gently fold the dough.

Carefully shape the dough into two oblong loaves.

Sourdough Bread with Green Tea

The green tea adds both richness and antioxidants to the bread.

Makes one loaf

1 cup (250 ml) strong green tea, lukewarm
7 oz (200 g) wheat sourdough starter (see page 20)
1 tbsp (15 g) salt
5 cups (600 g) wheat flour
olive oil for the bowl

Mix the ingredients and knead well. Let the dough rise in a greased and covered bowl for 1 hour.

Gently pour the dough onto a baking table. It should flow out slightly.

Gently fold the loaf and place it on a greased baking tray. Let it rise for another 30 minutes.

Initial Oven Temperature: 475°F (250°C)
Place the bread in the oven and sprinkle a cup of water on the bottom of the oven. Reduce the temperature to 400°F (200°C).

Bake the bread for about 25 minutes.

English Wheat Sourdough Bread

This bread is proof that English culinary traditions shouldn't be disparaged.

Makes 1 loaf

¾ oz (20 g) fresh yeast
1¼ cup (300 ml) water, room temperature
5½ cups (650 g) whole wheat flour
5 oz (150 g) wheat sourdough starter (see page 20)
1 tbsp (15 g) salt
1 tbsp raw sugar
¼ cup (50 ml) olive oil
melted butter for brushing

Dissolve the yeast in a little bit of the water. Mix all the ingredients thoroughly and knead well. If you need more water than what is specified, try adding a little at a time. The amount is only an approximation, as the responsiveness of the flour may vary.

Form the kneaded dough into a loaf and let it rise until it's doubled in volume, about 45–60 minutes. Brush a little melted butter on top of the bread before placing it in the oven.

Initial Oven Temperature: 450°F (230°C)
Place the bread in the oven and sprinkle a cup of water on the bottom of the oven. Reduce the temperature to 400°F (200°C).

Bake the bread for about 30 minutes.

Carrot Bread

The roasted oats give this bread a slightly nutty flavor, and the carrots make it juicy.

Makes 2–3 loaves

½ cup (100 ml) milk, room temperature
1¾ tsp (5 g) fresh yeast
1 tbsp (15 g) salt
3¾ cups (450 g) wheat flour, wholemeal
1 cup (100 g) rolled oats (dry roast them in a non-stick frying pan)
5 oz (150 g) wheat sourdough starter (see page 20)
1 cup (200 ml) water, room temperature
2 cups (250 g) grated carrots

Combine the milk and yeast. Mix all ingredients, except for the carrots. Knead the dough for about 10 minutes. Add the grated carrots and knead some more.

Let the dough rise for 60–90 minutes in a warm place.

Note that the dough will be slightly sticky. When the dough has risen fully, it should be kneaded again. Fill two to three greased pans halfway with dough. Let the dough rise for about 45 minutes. The actual time may vary slightly—the dough is ready when it has doubled in size.

Initial Oven Temperature: 475°F (250°C)
Place the loaves in the oven and bake for 10 minutes. Lower the temperature to 350°F (180°C) and bake for roughly 30 minutes more.

Roast the oats in a non-stick frying pan.

Knead the dough for about 10 minutes. Add the grated carrot.

Fill the pans halfway with the fermented and loose dough.

Rye Ciabatta

These loaves take some time to bake, but so much preparation makes for a pleasant taste.

Makes about 10 loaves

7 oz (200 g) wheat sourdough starter (see page 20)
½ cup (50 g) fine rye flour
4 cups (500 g) wheat flour
approx. 1²/₃ cups (400 ml) water, room temperature
½ tbsp (10 g) salt
olive oil for the bowl

Mix all the ingredients except the salt and knead well. Add the salt.

Place the dough in a greased mixing bowl. Cover with plastic film and let the dough stand in the refrigerator overnight.

The next day, gently pour the dough onto a baking table.

Fold the dough and let it sit in the refrigerator for approximately 5 hours, folding the dough again once each hour.

Pour the dough on the table. Cut it into pieces that are roughly 2 × 6 inches (10 × 15 cm) and place them on a greased baking sheet. Let them rise in the refrigerator for another 10 hours. This is why it takes about 2 days to make this bread.

Initial Oven Temperature: 475°F (250°C)
Place the loaves in the oven. Sprinkle a cup of water onto the floor of the oven. Reduce the temperature to 400°F (210°C) and bake for about 15 minutes.

Fold the dough and leave it in the fridge for about 5 hours. Repeat the folding once hour during this period of time.

Place the dough on the floured surface and stretch it out.

Cut the dough into pieces that are about 2 × 6 inches (10 × 15 cm).

Spelt Sourdough

This bread makes a wonderful hostess gift.

Makes 2 loaves

35 oz (1 kg) spelt sourdough starter (see page 20)
1 tbsp (15 g) salt
3 tbsp (25 g) fresh yeast
2½ tbsp (35 ml) treacle syrup (can be substituted with dark syrup)
½ cup (100 ml) water, room temperature
6 cups (625 g) fine rye flour
1¾ cup (225 g) wheat flour

Mix ingredients well and let rise for about 30 minutes.

Gently shape into two oblong loaves and sprinkle with flour. Let the bread rise until the loaves are doubled in size (let them rise in a basket, if possible).

Initial Oven Temperature: 475°F (250°C)
Place the loaves in the oven and sprinkle a cup of water on the floor of the oven. Reduce the temperature to 375°F (195°C).

Bake for about 30 minutes.

Olive Bread

Makes 2 loaves

10½ oz (300 g) spelt sourdough starter (see page 20)
6 cups (600 g) spelt flour, sifted
1¼ cup (300 ml) water, room temperature
1 tbsp honey
1 tbsp salt
⅔ cup (150 g) pitted olives, preferably a mix of green and black

Mix all the ingredients except for the olives. Knead thoroughly. The dough should be fairly "weak."

Flatten the dough into a "cake" that is 12 inches (30 cm) in diameter. Chop half of the olives. Add the chopped olives and mix in the whole olives. Roll up the dough and let rise for 2–3 hours. Cut the dough into 2 pieces and shape into loaves. Let the loaves rise for another 20 minutes.

Initial Oven Temperature: 475°F (250°C)
Place the bread in the oven and reduce temperature to 400°F (200°C). Bake for about 30–40 minutes.

Fold the dough over the olives.

After the dough has fermented for 2–3 hours, cut the dough in half.

Shape the bread so that the olive mixture is turned out.

French Peasant Bread

A rustic bread that's ideal to share at lengthy dinners.

Make 1 loaf

2 cups (500 ml) water, room temperature
5 cups (600 g) wheat flour
2 cups (200 g) spelt flour, sifted
4½ oz (125 g) wheat sourdough starter (see page 20)
4½ oz (125 g) rye sourdough starter (see page 20)
1½ tbsp (25 g) salt
olive oil for the bowl

Mix all the ingredients except the salt until the dough is smooth.

When the dough is well kneaded, add the salt. Continue kneading for another few minutes. Place the dough in a mixing bowl coated in oil, and cover with a cloth.

Let the dough rise for about 2 hours.

Pour the dough onto a floured table and shape into one long loaf. Let it rise for about 40 minutes.

Initial Oven Temperature: 525°F (270°C)
Place the bread in the oven and sprinkle a cup of water on the bottom of the oven. Reduce the temperature to 450°F (230°C).

Bake for about 30 minutes.

Bread with Rye Sourdough

Hazelnut Bread

This bread has a subtle richness.

Makes 2 loaves

2 cups (500 ml) water, room temperature
16 oz (450 g) rye sourdough starter (see page 20)
3¾ cups (450 g) wheat flour
2¼ cups (225 g) spelt flour, sifted
2¼ cups (225 g) fine rye flour
1½ tbsp (25 g) salt
2½ cups (350 g) whole hazelnuts
olive oil for the bowl

Mix together all the ingredients except for the salt and nuts. Knead the dough well.

Add the salt and nuts and knead into the dough.

Place the dough in a plastic mixing bowl coated in oil and let rise for about 3 hours.

Separate and shape the dough into 2 loaves and place them on a greased baking sheet. Let rise for another hour or so.

Initial Oven Temperature: 525°F (270°C)
Place the loaves in the oven and reduce the temperature to 450°F (230°C).

Bake the loaves for 30–40 minutes.

Russian Sweet Bread

With added toppings such as salami or cheese, this can be enjoyed as a meal in itself.

Makes 1 loaf

26½ oz (750 g) rye sourdough starter (see page 20)
1¼ cup (300 ml) water, room temperature
3½ tsp (20 g) salt
1 tbsp (10 g) caraway seeds
2½ cups (300 g) wheat flour
3 cups (300 g) spelt flour, sifted

Mix the ingredients and knead until the dough is smooth. Let it rise under a cloth for 1 hour.

Shape the dough into a large, round loaf. Place it on a greased baking sheet and cover with a cloth. Let the dough rise for 1–2 hours.

Before placing it in the oven, sprinkle the dough with flour. Bake in the oven at 400°F (210°C) for about 40–50 minutes.

Danish Rye Bread

The perfect breakfast bread to wake up every cell in your body.

Makes 3 loaves

Day 1
2 cups (500 ml) water, room temperature
3 cups (300 g) whole grain rye flour
1 oz (25 g) rye sourdough starter (see page 20)

Mix the ingredients well and let stand at room temperature overnight.

Day 2
4 cups (1 liter) water, room temperature
8 cups (800 g) whole grain rye flour
2 cups (250 g) whole wheat flour
2 tbsp (35 g) salt
4½ oz (125 g) sunflower seeds
4½ oz (125 g) pumpkin seeds
2½ oz (75 g) whole flaxseed

Combine the dough made the previous day with the new ingredients. Mix thoroughly for about 10 minutes.

Divide the dough into three 8 × 4 × 3 inch (1½ liter) loaf pans. The pans should be filled only two thirds of the way. Let it rise in a warm place for 3–4 hours.

Initial Oven Temperature: 475°F (250°C)
Place the pans in the oven and reduce the temperature to 350°F (180°C). Sprinkle a cup of water on the floor of the oven. Bake the loaves for 40–50 minutes.

Day 2: Mix the remaining ingredients with the starter.

Stir the dough well for about 10 minutes.

Place the dough in an 8 × 4 × 3 inch loaf pan (1 1/2 liters). Fill the pan no more than two-thirds of the way to the top. Let rise until the dough has reached the edge of the pan.

Walnut Bread

This bread makes a wonderful complement to mature cheeses.

Makes 1 loaf

2 cups (500 ml) water, room temperature
14 oz (400 g) rye sourdough starter (see page 20)
4 cups (400 g) unmixed rye flour (i.e. without wheat flour)
4 cups (500 g) wheat flour
14 oz (400 g) whole walnuts
3½ tsp (20 g) salt
olive oil for the bowl

Mix all the ingredients except for the walnuts and salt. Knead until the dough is smooth.

Once the dough is well kneaded, add the salt and walnuts. Continue kneading for another few minutes. Then, place the dough in an oiled mixing bowl and cover it with a cloth.

Let the dough rise for about 2 hours.

Place the dough on a floured surface and shape it into one round loaf. Let it rise on a greased baking sheet for about 30 minutes.

Initial Oven Temperature: 475°F (250°C)
Place the bread in the oven and sprinkle a cup of water on the bottom of the oven. Reduce the temperature to 450°F (230°C).

Bake the bread for about 30 minutes.

Once the dough is well kneaded, add the salt and walnuts. Knead again for a few minutes.

After the dough has risen, cut it into two pieces.

Flatten out the pieces slightly on the baking sheet.

Spelt Bread with Orange

The orange peel suits the natural acidity of the bread.

Makes 1 loaf

Step 1
½ of a regular-sized orange

Peel the orange. Simmer the peel in water for a few minutes. Remove from the water and let it cool slightly.

Using a spoon, scrape away the white part on the inside of the peel. Chop the peel into small pieces.

Step 2
orange peel pieces
7 oz (200 g) rye sourdough starter (see page 20)
1 cup (200 ml) water, room temperature
½ tbsp (10 g) salt
1 tsp (5 g) fennel
approximately 6–7 cups (600–700 g) spelt flour, sifted

Mix all the ingredients, but add the last few cups of flour slowly. Spelt flour doesn't absorb liquid in the same way as regular wheat flour. Knead well.

Let the dough rise for about 30 minutes.

Shape the dough into a round loaf and place on a greased baking sheet. Let the dough rise until it has doubled in size; this can take up to a few hours.

Bake at 400°F (200°C) for about 25 minutes.

Brush the bread with water after removing it from the oven.

Anise Bread

This anise bread is a perfect Christmas loaf.

Makes 1 loaf

3 cups (300 g) finely ground rye flour
2½ cups (250 g) spelt flour, sifted
10½ oz (300 g) rye sourdough starter (see page 20)
½ tbsp (10 g) salt
4 tsp (20 g) raw sugar
1¼ cup (300 ml) beer with a low alcohol content, room temperature
½ oz (15 g) crushed anise
1¾ oz (50 g) flaxseed

Mix all the ingredients. The dough will be quite sticky. Let sit at room temperature for about 1 hour.

Lightly flour your hands and gently knead the dough. Shape the dough into a large, round bun and place on a greased baking sheet.

Let the bread rise until it has doubled in size. This may take a couple of hours.

Initial Oven Temperature: 450°F (230°C)
Place the bread in the oven and sprinkle a cup of water on the bottom. Reduce the temperature to 350°F (180°C) and bake for 45–55 minutes.

Sunflower Bread

A wonderful alternative to ordinary dinner rolls.

Makes about 15–20 rolls

1¾ tsp (5 g) fresh yeast
1¼ cup (300 ml) water, room temperature
3 cups (300 g) finely ground rye flour
2½ cups (300 g) wheat flour
7 oz (200 g) rye sourdough starter (see page 20)
1 tbsp (15 g) salt
3 tbsp (50 g) honey
⅔ cup (150 ml) sunflower seeds
1 tbsp (10 g) cumin

Dissolve the yeast in a little bit of the water. Add all ingredients and mix well.

Let the dough rise in a warm place until it has doubled in size. This will take 1–2 hours.

Shape the dough into fifteen to twenty small rolls. Place them on a greased baking sheet and let them rise in a warm place until doubled in size.

Bake at 350°F (180°C) for about 10 minutes.

Knead the dough after it has risen, and shape into a long roll.

Cut the dough into fifteen to twenty pieces.

Shape into round loaves and place on a baking sheet to rise until doubled in size.

Beer Bread

This is an acidic German bread. A piece of cheese or a pat of butter makes for a sensual complement.

Makes 2 loaves

approximately 1¼ cup (300 ml) beer, room temperature
7 tsp (20 g) fresh yeast
1 tbsp (15 g) salt
16 oz (450 g) rye sourdough starter (see page 20)
5½ cups (700 g) whole wheat flour

Mix together all the ingredients, except for the flour. Add the flour a little at a time and mix well. Don't add all the flour at once; test the dough to ensure that it is elastic before adding more flour. Knead well.

Let the dough rest for about 15 minutes. Knead well.

Shape the dough into two loaves and let rise on a greased baking sheet until it has roughly doubled in size. Sprinkle a little flour over the bread.

Initial Oven Temperature: 475°F (250°C)
Place the loaves in the oven and sprinkle a cup of water on the bottom. Lower the temperature to 400°F (200°C).

Bake the bread for about 45 minutes.

Crispy Bread

Crispy Rye Bread

Crispy bread that will remind you of times past.

Makes about 20 crackers

17½ oz (500 g) rye sourdough starter made from whole wheat
   rye flour (see page 20)
17½ oz (500 g) wheat sourdough starter (see page 20)
5 cups (500 g) fine rye flour
½ tbsp (10 g) salt

Mix the ingredients well and let the dough rise for about 2 hours.

Roll the dough out as thinly as possible. Cut into crackers and place on a greased baking sheet. Prick with a fork to keep the bread from bubbling.

Let the crackers rise for 2–3 hours.

Bake at 400°F (210°C) for roughly 10 minutes.

Tasty Crispy Bread

A great feature at Mardi Gras and Christmas parties.

Makes 15 crackers

½ oz (10 g) fresh yeast
1²/₃ cups (400 ml) cold water
3½ oz (100 g) rye sourdough starter (see page 20)
3½ oz (100 g) wheat sourdough starter (see page 20)
3 cups (300 g) whole rye flour
4¼ cups (550 g) wheat flour
1 tbsp (15 g) salt
½ oz (15 g) anise
sea salt for topping

Dissolve the yeast in the water and mix with the sourdough. Add the flour and knead thoroughly. Let the dough rest for about 15 minutes.

Add salt and anise and knead the dough once more. Place in a bowl covered with plastic wrap. Let it rise in the refrigerator overnight.

The next day, cut the dough into fifteen pieces. Roll each piece of dough out until it becomes a thin cracker. To keep the dough from sticking, lightly flour the rolling pin. Occasionally turn the cracker over to ensure that you're spreading the dough out properly.

Place the crackers on a baking sheet covered in parchment paper. Prick them with a fork. Sprinkle with a little sea salt according to taste.

Bake the crackers at about 400°F (210°C) for 15 minutes. Let the crackers dry on a cooling rack.

Shape the dough into rolls and cut it into fifteen pieces.

Roll each piece of dough into a thin wafer. Lightly coat the dough with flour to prevent it from sticking to the rolling pin.

Prick the crackers with a fork. Sprinkle with sea salt and place on a sheet covered with parchment paper.

Thin Crackers

The ever-popular cracker.

Makes 6–8 large crackers

¾ cup (200 ml) high-fat yogurt
7 oz (200 g) rye sourdough starter (see page 20)
2 tsp (15 g) honey
½ tbsp (10 g) salt
4 cups (500 g) wheat flour

Mix all the ingredients and knead the dough thoroughly.

Cut the dough into six to eight round pieces. Roll the pieces into thin wafers. Lightly flour the surface and the dough to prevent the dough from sticking. Place the crackers on a greased baking sheet and prick them with a fork.

Bake the crackers at 430°F (220°C) for about 10 minutes. Let them dry on a cooling rack.

Roll the dough into a long cylinder and cut it into six to eight pieces.

Roll the dough as thin as possible.

Prick with a fork.

Sourdough Breads with Oats, Potatoes, and Lentils

Oat Bread

Makes 3 loaves

1 batch of oat sourdough starter (see page 23)
½ cup (125 ml) water, room temperature
½ tbsp (10 g) salt
2 tsp (15 g) honey
approx. 2½ cups (300 g) wheat flour
a few rolled oats

Mix all ingredients except the rolled oats and knead well. Let the dough rise for 2–3 hours.

Shape the dough into three round loaves. Brush with water and dip the bread in the rolled oats. Let the dough rise on a greased baking sheet for another 45 minutes.

Bake the loaves at 375°F (190°C) for roughly 20 minutes.

Potato Bread

Makes 1 loaf

Step 1 (pre-dough)
1 batch of potato sourdough starter (see page 23)
2 cups (250 g) wheat flour
1¾ oz (50 g) rosehip shells

Combine the sourdough and flour and let stand in the refrigerator for about 8 hours.

Soak the rosehip shells in a separate bowl.

Step 2
¾ cup (200 ml) water, room temperature
½ tbsp (10 g) salt
½ cup (50 g) finely ground rye flour
2 cups (200 g) spelt flour, sifted

Remove the pre-dough from the refrigerator. Add the ingredients listed above, plus the drained rosehip shells.

Knead the dough well and shape into a loaf. Place on a greased baking sheet and let rise under a cloth until it's doubled in size. This can take a few hours.

Bake the bread at 400°F (200°C) for about 25 minutes.

Lentil Bread

Makes 1 loaf

1 batch of lentil sourdough starter (see page 24)
¼ cup (50 g) olive oil
2 tsp (10 g) sea salt
½ cup (100 ml) water, room temperature
2 cups (250 g) wheat flour

Mix the ingredients and knead well. If the dough is too loose, then add a little more flour. Place the dough in the refrigerator overnight.

Remove the dough and knead it a little more. Shape the dough into a loaf and place on a greased baking sheet.

Let the bread rise in the refrigerator for about 12 hours.

Remove the bread from the refrigerator and let it stand at room temperature for 30 minutes before putting it in the oven. Bake the bread at 400°F (200°C) for about 30 minutes.

Sweet Sourdough Bread

Karlsbad Bread

Makes about 30 buns

1²⁄₃ cups (400 ml) milk, room temperature
7 oz (200 g) wheat sourdough starter (see page 20)
9 cups (1 kg) wheat flour
3½ tbsp (30 g) fresh yeast
1 cup (250 g) butter
1 cup (200 g) sugar
6 egg yolks
½ tbsp (10 g) salt
1 egg for brushing

Mix 1¼ cup (300 ml) of the milk with the sourdough, half of the flour, and the yeast. Let it rise for about 1 hour.

Melt the butter and let it cool.

Mix all the ingredients with the dough. Knead the dough until smooth.

Shape the dough into thirty or so plain buns or crescents and place them on a greased baking sheet. Let them rise under a cloth until the buns have doubled in size.

Brush the buns with the beaten egg. Bake at 400°F (210°C) for about 10 minutes.

Gugelhupf

A classic German cake made with stirred wheat dough.

Makes 1–2 cakes

Step 1

1¾ tsp (5 g) fresh yeast
1 cup (250 ml) milk, room temperature
3 cups (375 g) wheat flour
3½ oz (100 g) wheat sourdough starter (see page 20)

Dissolve the yeast in a little of the milk. Add the other ingredients and mix well. Let the dough rise for 1–2 hours.

Step 2

1 cup (200 ml) milk, room temperature
3¾ cups (450 g) wheat flour
½ cup (100 g) sugar
¾ cup (175 g) melted butter, cooled
3–4 eggs
zest from 1 lemon
1 cup (150 g) raisins
powdered sugar for garnish

Add all ingredients to the dough and mix thoroughly. Fill one or two greased and floured 11 × 7 × 1 ½ inch Bundt pans (1 ½ liter) halfway with dough. Let the dough rise until it is about 30 percent larger, or for 1 hour.

Bake at 390°F (200°C) for 20–30 minutes. Let the cake cool before removing it from the pan. Lastly, sprinkle with the powdered sugar.

Mix the dough with the ingredients from step two and stir well.

Fill the greased and floured molds halfway with dough.

Let the baked cake cool before slicing.

Brioche

Makes about 20 rolls

3½ oz (100 g) wheat sourdough starter (see page 20)
3½ cups (450 g) wheat flour
⅓ cup (75 ml) milk, room temperature
5¼ tsp (15 g) fresh yeast
5 eggs
⅓ cup (75 g) sugar
1½ tbsp (25 g) salt
1½ cup (350 g) unsalted butter, softened
1 egg for brushing

Mix the sourdough with half of the wheat flour, the milk, and the yeast. Let the mixture rise for about 2 hours.

Add all the ingredients except the butter and mix thoroughly. Then, add the butter little by little—about ¼ cup (50 g) at a time. Knead well.

Cover with a cloth and let the dough rise for about 30 minutes.

Shape into twenty small, smooth buns. Place them in cupcake molds and let rise until they have doubled in size. Brush the buns with the egg.

Bake the brioche at 400°F (210°C) for about 10 minutes.

Wheat Buns

This recipe can be used to make buns and braided wreaths.

Makes about 35 buns

2 cups (500 ml) milk, room temperature
1¾ oz (50 g) wheat sourdough starter (see page 20)
9½ cups (1¼ kg) wheat flour
1 cup (200 g) butter
½ cup (75 g) fresh yeast
½ cup (165 g) white syrup
½ oz (15 g) ground cardamom
1 tsp (5 g) salt
1 egg for brushing
pearl sugar for garnish

Mix 1⅔ cup (400 ml) of the milk with the sourdough and half of the flour. Let rise for about 1 hour.

Melt the butter and let cool.

Dissolve the yeast in the remaining milk. When done, add all the ingredients into the first dough and mix thoroughly. Knead until smooth.

Shape the dough into thirty-five buns and place them on a greased baking sheet. Let them rise under a cloth until they have doubled in size.

Brush the buns with the beaten egg and sprinkle with a little pearl sugar. Bake at 400°F (210°C) for about 10 minutes.

Index

Opposite page, top left: French Peasant Bread, recipe page 48. Top right: Wheat Buns, recipe page 85. Bottom right: Italiano, recipe page 28.

Acknowledgments

Many thanks to Bacchus Antiques, Bruka, Evensen Antik, Granite, and Mio City in Stockholm for lending us all the beautiful objects for the photo shoots!